ACKNOWLEDGEMENT

Now that I am eighty years old, I realize that there are not many people left who know how it was to be a child growing up in the early 1900s on a ranch in northern California. This way of life on a ranch is a part of our history and is the reason I wrote this story.

I wanted to tell my children, my grandchildren, and other children about Rainbow Ranch. I wanted people to know that underneath the deep waters of Lake Siskiyou, there was once a beautiful ranch where I was born. This is why I tell my grandchildren that their grandmother was born under water.

Two years ago my four children gave me, much to my surprise, a computer. I have had no lessons, and I am slowly learning to use it. Having a computer also encouraged me to write this story. I thank my children, Judy Kennedy, Sue Doyle, Kathleen McLeary, and Steve Price, for making this story possible, because without a computer this story would only have remained an unfilled dream.

A special thanks to my publisher, Shari Fiock. This book was "finished" several times, but than new ideas would surface, and Shari was always there with her patience and enthusiasm.

Thanks to my daughter, Judy Kennedy, who helped me with the final editing and proofreading. Her 32-years as a fourth grade teacher helped me see my story through a child's eye.

Thanks to "Bud" Goodrich, who read the first chapters and encouraged me to continue writing my book.

Clelia (Kay) Price

RAINBOW RANCH   circa 1965

RAINBOW RANCH

Grandma Tabby is excited, because her three grandkittens, Blackie, Calico, and Patches would be arriving for several weeks. The kittens live in the city, but they come for vacations with their owner who has a cottage not far from where Tabby now lives.

Grandma is taking a nap when the kittens arrive. They all crowd around her, and after many licks and much purring, Grandma Tabby tells the kittens how well they look and how much each has grown. Finally they ask, "Will you tell us a story?" They loved Grandma's stories.

Blackie asks for the story of Rainbow Ranch, which is one of their favorites. They all know about the beautiful area where Grandma had once lived, and they know that the ranch had been flooded and no longer exists.

Before she can start her story, Patches, who always wants to know every detail, asks, "Why was it called Rainbow Ranch?"

"As you all know," said Grandma Tabby, "the ranch was in a valley covered with trees and green alfalfa fields, and after a rain a beautiful rainbow would arch across the entire valley."

"But Grandma," said Calico who knew all the Bible stories, "you said that the ranch was flooded, but God told Noah after he had sent the flood to wipe out all the wicked people that he would not send another flood. As a sign he put his bow in the sky, and we call it a rainbow."

"Why Calico!" said Grandma, "I am so pleased that you remember the Bible stories I told you. It was not God who flooded the ranch, but some people who lived in a town called Sacramento that caused the ranch to be under water. As representatives of the State of California, they said it had to be done so that the Sacramento River would not flood the nearby towns.

"When they heard this was going to happen, everyone at the ranch was sad. They could not believe it would really happen, but happen it did. Many people came to work on the dam. They made lots of noise, and it took many years to build."

"I bet it was sad for you too, Grandma," said Patches, "to see all the fields covered with water in the places where you used to catch fat mice."

"Yes, we were all sad."

This hadn't been a happy story, and the kittens sat quietly. They knew Grandma had many stories, and not all of them were sad.

Grandma continued "When the dam was being built, Kay, who was the little girl who had lived on the ranch, came from the city where she lived as a young adult, to see the ranch one more time. She met the man whose job it was to cut down all the trees and burn the ranch buildings to make way for the lake. The man told her that there were so many ugly things in this world. Yet here was a beautiful ranch, and it was his job to destroy it." Grandma closed her eyes, and the kittens knew it was time to leave.

The kittens were silent and thoughtful on their way home.

THE RATTLESNAKE SCARE

On their next visit, the kittens gathered cozily around Grandma Tabby to hear another story. The kittens said, "Tell us about Kay." They all knew this was Grandma's favorite story.

Kay was the little girl who lived on the ranch, and Grandma Tabby used to follow her everywhere. The kittens knew most of the stories, but they loved to hear them again and again.

"Tell us about the big rattlesnake," said Blackie. This was the favorite of all the stories.

Grandma began her story, "I was sitting in the big oak tree just outside the cellar door."

"What is a cellar?" asked Patches.

"The cellar was an important place. A long time ago there were no refrigerators or freezers. The food was kept in the cellar which was a large room dug under the house. It had no windows, and it was cool enough to keep the food from spoiling, even on a hot summer day."

"But Grandma, you said you would tell us the snake story," said Blackie.

"Right you are Blackie. As I was saying, I was in the oak tree. Kay was about ten years old at the time. She and her four-year-old cousin, Denzi, had come to get some food from the cellar. There by the cellar door was a coiled rattlesnake. I saw the snake, but Kay did not."

Grandma went on, "This was one time I wished I could speak like a person. If only I could warn her. '*Oh, please look down,*' I thought. Kay was very close to the snake. If she had taken one more step the coiled snake would have been within striking distance, but she stopped just in time. Kay's eyes were wide, and her hands shook as she shoved Denzi behind her. Slowly she backed away."

"My," said Calico, "she was a brave little girl."

"Yes, she was," said Grandma. "I could see how frightened she was. She could not call her Papa, because he had gone to town to deliver the milk. Her step-mother was a strange lady, for whenever she saw a snake of any kind she would scream. Her screams were so loud that they could be heard all over the ranch. Kay knew she would not get any help from her. Luckily, a hoe was close by, and she got it and quickly chopped off the snake's head."

There was a big sigh from the three kittens as they stopped holding their breath. This had been a long story, and the kittens were ready to play. Grandma said, "I am really tired, and it is time for my nap."

THE BABY BIRD RESCUE

Blackie, Patches, and Calico arrived early to see Grandma Tabby. It was a lovely day. The apple trees had lots of busy bees going from blossom to blossom gathering nectar to make the honey we all liked.

"May we have a story?" asked the kittens. They hoped it would be about Kay, for they knew how much Grandma loved her. Grandma Tabby nodded and began her story.

"It was a day very much like today. I was in the orchard hoping to find a baby bird for a meal. I heard some chirping and crept toward the sound, but as I came near I saw Kay pick up the baby bird and put it in her pocket. Then she looked up at the apple tree, and she saw the nest from which the bird had fallen. Kay held onto a branch and pulled herself up into the tree. I could see her put the baby robin, that would have been my meal, carefully back into its nest. As she was climbing down from the tree, her dress caught on a limb, and she fell, and I heard her cry out. Her arm was at a strange angle, because she had broken it at the elbow."

Patches interrupted. "Why was she wearing a dress? If she had been wearing jeans, she probably would not have fallen."

"That's right Patches, but a long time ago little girls did not wear long pants, and jeans were only worn by boys."

Grandma continued, "Her Papa took her to the only doctor in town who was not a very good doctor. You should have heard some of the stories people told about him. When Kay's arm healed, it was crooked. In order to straighten it, the doctor had her carry a pail of sand as a weight for half-a-mile every day. I always walked with her, but I could see that this strange treatment was not helping her arm.

"One day, Chris, Kay's cousin, was visiting. They were playing horse. Chris was holding one end of the rope, and Kay, acting as the horse, was holding the other end. They were running fast when he yelled, 'Whoa,' but Kay didn't stop galloping. The rope jerked, and her arm was yanked very hard. All of a sudden I heard her say with great excitement, 'My arm is straight!' Everyone was happy to see that her arm was normal again."

SHEP AND THE PORCUPINE

The kittens were awake early. After breakfast, they left to see Grandma. She was asleep near their friend, Sammy, the old dog who never bothered them. Grandma woke up and stretched, looked at Sammy, and began to tell them another story.

"We had many dogs on the ranch, but Shep was a special friend of mine. He came to the ranch when he was a puppy, and everyone thought he was very strange, because he had one blue eye and one brown eye.

"After we had become good friends, I asked Shep about his eyes. He said everyone in his family had one blue eye and one brown eye. They came from a faraway land called Australia, and they were called Australian shepherds. Shep said his grandparents worked on large sheep ranches. They helped the sheepherder take care of his sheep. I then knew why Shep was so good with the cows on our ranch. Kay would ride Dolly, her horse, and Shep was always there to help her herd the cows to the barn.

"Sometimes Shep got into trouble. There were many porcupines on the ranch. Kay's Papa would get cross when they trampled the alfalfa fields."

"What is a porcupine?" asked Blackie.

Grandma said, "I forgot that you kittens have never seen one. Porcupines are rodents. Their bodies are covered with thousands of long, sharp quills or spines.

"Shep also didn't like porcupines, and he would try to bite them, and the quills which were like sharp needles would stick in his nose. This was very painful for Shep. Kay's brother, Joe, had to use pliers to remove the quills from Shep's nose.

"You would think that would be a lesson for Shep, but he never did learn to leave porcupines alone."

RAINBOW RANCH GUIDES THE PLANE

The kittens wondered what Grandma Tabby would tell them today. She started her story as soon as they were settled.

"A long time ago everyone had chores to do at the ranch. Even Kay was kept busy. Of all her chores, the one she disliked the most was cleaning the chimneys of the kerosene lamps. Every morning she used an old newspaper to remove the soot from the glass chimneys. Her stepmother was never pleased with her work and would make her do it over until they were shining. Kay's Papa hated to see his little girl unhappy.

"I had heard everyone talking about having their own electricity, and one day Kay's Papa laid pipes from their irrigation ditch down the hill to the dairy. The power from the water turned the generator, and there was electricity. Kay was happy, for she no longer had to clean the chimneys of the kerosene lamps.

"I didn't understand how it works, but the electrical current was direct. This meant that not too many lights could be turned off, or the motor would get hot. The only lights turned off were the ones in the bedrooms. All day and all night the lights were on in the barn, in the dairy, and in the house.

"The mail plane, which flew over the ranch every morning at 4:00 A.M., carried the mail from Portland to San Francisco. The plane would use the lights of the ranch as a beacon. When it was stormy, the lone pilot in his small single-engine plane felt comfort in seeing the lights of Rainbow Ranch, and knowing he was on course. The only time the lights were turned off was during the war, and our government wanted all lights turned out for they could have served as a beacon for the enemy planes.

"During the war Kay was living on a hill overlooking San Francisco. When the siren blew, everyone knew it was a blackout and all the lights had to be turned off. Her little girl, Judy, would look out the window to watch as all the lights of the city turned off. Where minutes before there had been hundreds of lights now was total darkness. Kay said it was frightening, because no one knew what would happen. They all knew about the bombing of Pearl Harbor. What a relief it was for everyone when the all clear sign would sound and San Francisco was again sparkling with lights."

The kittens felt safe and happy now that there were no more enemies to worry about.

BABY CHICKS ARRIVE IN THE MAIL

As Blackie, Patches, and Calico walked toward Grandma Tabby's house, they kept guessing as to what the story would be about today. Each story she told them was exciting and fun. The kittens were learning about a way of life that was unusual and interesting to them.

Grandma Tabby wasted no time, for she knew that the kittens would be leaving soon, and there were so many things she wanted them to learn about her life with Kay.

"I am sure you know about catalogs. The mail is full of all kinds of catalogs. There are so many they have become a nuisance. Many years ago it was a special day when the Montgomery Ward and Sears Roebuck catalogs arrived. Almost everything Kay and her family needed came from the catalog. The catalogs were like a miniature shopping mall. Instead of walking around and looking, you turned the pages of the catalog. There were thousands of items to choose from. It was also called the Wish Book, for one could say, 'I wish I could order that.' If you saw the boys in the corner looking at the catalog and giggling, they were probably looking at the pages with the women's underwear.

"As soon as the new winter catalog arrived, the summer catalog, which only a few months ago had held a place of honor, would be used in the outhouse for toilet paper."

"What is an outhouse?" asked Calico.

Grandma said, "I think I told you that a long time ago there were no bathrooms in the house and the toilets were outside in a very small house. It was not an especially pleasant place and you did what you needed to do and left."

Grandma continued her story, "One day Kay was excited, because a notice came in the mail informing them that the little chicks, which had been ordered from the catalog, had arrived. She and her Papa went to the post office, and there on the shelves were boxes and boxes of chirping baby chicks. Kay's Papa took the two boxes with a dozen little chicks in each and carefully carried them to the truck. The chicks looked like balls of soft yellow cotton. Kay sat in the back to make sure the boxes would stay upright.

"Once the chicks arrived at the ranch, they were kept in boxes behind the stove where they would stay warm. I was not allowed in the house during this time. I don't think Kay trusted me with the baby chicks. One would have made me a good meal. It was Kay's job to see that they always had fresh water, and she fed them finely mashed egg yolks. When the chicks were old enough to take care of themselves, they would be put in the chicken house with the other chickens."

COYOTES IN THE CHICKEN HOUSE

Then Grandma told them something else about the chicken house. "There were many coyotes that lived near the ranch and almost every night you could hear their howls. Coyotes liked chickens and sometimes they would try and get in the hen house. What excitement that caused! The dogs would bark, the chickens would squawk, and Kay's Papa would grab his shotgun and run to the chicken house. The coyotes were very smart, because as soon as they smelled a human they would run away. Kay's Papa never did catch them."

Blackie said, "What fun it must have been to be part of the excitement."

WASHING ON THE RANCH

Every time Calico, Blackie, and Patches were going to see Grandma, they licked and cleaned themselves. Grandma always checked to see if they were neat and clean. Her story today was about keeping clean on the ranch.

"As I told you before, houses did not have a bathroom. Kay had to wash her hands in a basin on the back porch. The water was ice cold, because it came from the nearby snow covered mountains. It felt good in summer but not in the winter. Kay took her bath once a week, generally on Saturday night. The water was heated on the wood stove and poured into a large washtub that was on the kitchen floor near the stove. How wonderful Kay felt to scrub herself clean.

"In the summer, a bath in the washtub wasn't necessary, because the Sacramento River was nearby. Joe, Kay's brother, with help from his cousin, Chris, would dam the river with large boulders until the river formed a large swimming pool. The dam was washed away every winter by the swift waters, but come summer the boys would rebuild it. A diving board was made by using a long plank of wood anchored with a large boulder.

"Kay's girl cousins, Eda, and Anita, came often to swim and play in the river. Of course the water was ice cold, but on a hot day everyone seemed to like it. I would sit in a tree close by and watch them swim and have fun."

Grandma Tabby continued her story. "Since clothes washers and dryers had not been invented, the clothes were washed in a large metal washtub. They were scrubbed on a washboard which was a wooden board with metal ridges. Washing clothes this way was indeed hard work. Then the clothes were hung outdoors on the clothesline to dry.

"We loved watching the clothes blow in the wind. The overalls danced and flapped in the breeze. Kay's little dresses twirled to a music of their own. In winter the clothes froze and Papa's overalls became so stiff, they looked as if he were in them. At sunset the clothes would be taken indoors. Kay was too small to do this, but her older sisters, Mary and Inez, stacked the frozen clothes on their arms like pieces of wood. The clothes were put around the wood stove to thaw and finish drying."

PATCHES AND THE PROSCIUTTO

Calico, Patches, and Blackie were late for their promised visit with Grandma Tabby, so she climbed a knoll to wait for them. She was pleased when she saw them, but she noticed that they were walking slowly, and Patches was limping. Grandma rushed to meet them and asked what had happened.

Everyone started talking at the same time, until Patches said, "Wait a minute, this is my story. Let me tell Grandma what happened." The other two kittens became quiet.

Patches began her story: "Do you know Claire, the little girl I live with?"

Grandma Tabby nodded. She was happy that the kittens had a nice family to live with; Claire reminded her of Kay who used to live on the ranch.

"Yesterday, Claire's mother was giving a party. She had been working in the kitchen all morning, and Claire and I were in her way, so we were told to go outside and not bother her.

"After awhile, no sounds came from the kitchen, so Claire knew her mother had gone upstairs. Claire wanted some of the melon that her mother had been cutting into small slices. She quietly went into the kitchen and took some melon from the refrigerator. The melon slices had thin pieces of ham wrapped around them. Claire didn't like the ham, so she gave me several pieces. It was delicious. Just then Claire's mother came downstairs where we were. When she saw me eating the ham, she became very upset, because Claire had taken some of the special food that was for her party. She cried out, 'Do you know how much I paid for the ham that you gave to that cat? Go to your room and stay there,' she said to Claire.

"I know she didn't mean to really hurt me," said Patches, "but she had a broom in her hand and swept me off the porch. I landed on my shoulder, and it hurt."

"My poor Patches," said Grandma, licking the kitten's shoulder, "I hope it doesn't hurt too much.

"I know what you were eating. It is called prosciutto. Kay's Papa was noted for making excellent prosciutto. In the cellar at the ranch there were several of these hams. Kay used to cut big slices and put them on home baked bread. She and I would sit under the oak tree and have a feast."

Grandma went on, "Let me tell you about the butchering of the pigs at the ranch. First of all, the pigs had to be fat. In the fall one of our jobs was to collect acorns for them to eat. Kay would take her red wagon, and I would sit in it. We went along until we found a grove of oak trees, and then we would fill the wagon with acorns."

"But Grandma, you are a cat, and you can't pick up acorns," said Blackie.

"I didn't actually pick them up, but I watched Kay do it. The acorns were then ground up and mixed with mash and fed to the pigs.

"You should see all the things that were made from the pig. First of all, there was the wonderful prosciutto. Then there was another type of ham, and also sausage, salami, and bacon.

"What Kay and I liked best of all was the balloon which her Papa gave us. It was the pig's bladder, and it made a very strong balloon that lasted for many months. It wasn't like the modern balloons that pop easily."

The kittens had heard many stories, but they had never heard of a balloon that was made from a pig's bladder.

HOMEMADE ICE CREAM

As the kittens walked to Grandma Tabby's house, they were discussing which of the many stories she had told them was the best.

Blackie quickly said, "I like the rattlesnake story."

Patches thought a moment and said, "My favorite is about the coyotes who tried to get in the hen house."

After a long silence, Calico said, "It seems that the last story Grandma tells us is always the best, so I don't think I have a favorite. I like them all."

Grandma Tabby felt a sense of urgency, for soon the kittens would be leaving, and there was so much she wanted them to know.

"A long time ago it was not possible to have store bought ice cream for dessert. If you were lucky enough to arrive with it unmelted, there was no freezer to keep it frozen. If you wanted ice cream you had to make your own.

"The ranch had a three-gallon ice cream maker. The rich cream from the cows, and the fresh eggs from the chickens, would be used to make a light custard, which was then put in the springhouse where the cold water cooled it. After it was chilled, the custard was put in the container and ice and rock salt were placed around the outer edge of the metal container."

Calico interrupted, "In summer, where did they get the ice?"

Grandma said, "During the winter, Kay's Papa would take the sled with a team of horses and go to a nearby frozen lake and saw huge blocks of ice. It was stored in the ice house which had double walls filled with sawdust for insulation, so the ice blocks would not melt."

She continued her story. "Kay always wanted to be the first to turn the ice cream handle because it was easy to turn when it was liquid. As it hardened she was no longer able to turn the handle, but there were many hands ready to take over the job. Ice cream was difficult to make with just a few people. It worked best if it was a group effort. When no one could turn the ice cream handle it was ready.

"When the beater was taken out of the container, a great deal of ice cream was left on it. The beater was scraped and given to Kay who would eat what was left, and then she would let me lick it clean. How wonderful it tasted, so cool and creamy."

The kittens licked their lips; they could almost taste the rich, creamy ice cream.

Grandma continued, "The container with the ice cream was then covered with more rock salt and ice and left to set.

"Then the children would go and find their favorite toppings. In the garden they picked the sweet, ripe, juicy strawberries — not like the ones you buy in stores that are often tasteless. Kay's favorite was the raspberries that grew on the fence. If someone was lucky they could go to the orchard and find a sun-ripened peach.

"When the ice cream was ready it was such a feast. Everyone had all they could eat."

THE GANDER GETS DRUNK

Calico could tell by the look in Grandma's eyes that this was going to be a funny story. "On the ranch was a flock of geese. The gander did not like Kay, and every chance he had he would chase her, trying to nip her legs. The gander did not bother anyone else, only Kay. It got so that she did not want to go outdoors. She would watch from the window, and when she was sure the gander was nowhere in sight, she would venture out. The gander would be watching, too. He would wait until she was quite a distance from the house and then take off after her. It was so funny to see this little girl running as fast as her short legs could go with the gander, its wings flapping, in hot pursuit. The gander's behavior ended in a strange way.

"Kay's Papa made his own wine. After the juice to make wine was removed, the remains of the grapes would be put outside in a pile. In a few days they would ferment. One day the gander thought he would eat some. He became so drunk that he could hardly stand, and his proud neck dangled. How Kay laughed, because in his condition he was no threat to her. After this embarrassing experience the gander no longer chased her."

TEACHING A CALF TO DRINK

Grandma had another tale to tell. "In the springtime there were many calves born on the ranch. The calves were not allowed to nurse for very long, because the milk was needed to sell to the customers. They had to be taught to drink milk on their own, and this is how Kay taught them to drink.

"Kay would get a bucket of skim milk with mash in it. She would put her fingers in the calf's mouth, and it would begin sucking on her fingers. Next she would lower her fingers slowly into the bucket of skim milk and gently remove her fingers from the calf's mouth. The calf would continue to suck, but instead of sucking her fingers he was drinking milk on his own." The kittens thought, "What a clever girl was their Grandma's friend."

SEASONS ON THE RANCH

When they arrived at Grandma Tabby's house they spent some quality time purring together before she started her story.

"Rainbow Ranch had four definite seasons and each one was special. Spring was a time to enjoy the warmth of the sun after a cold winter. It was a busy time. The large garden was plowed and the vegetables were planted, for there had to be enough vegetables for the family to eat all year."

Blackie interrupted, "They didn't have to go to the store every day?"

"No," said Grandma, "and when they did buy the few staples they needed, like flour, it was purchased in one hundred pound sacks. Several loaves of bread were baked twice a week. Nothing was wasted, even the flour sacks were used as dish cloths. The feathers from the chickens were made into bed pillows. The sheep were shorn in the spring, and the wool was carded to make warm comforters for winter use." Grandma paused, "All the meat for the dinner table came from the ranch. This may sound wonderful to have everything you need, but it took the women many hours to do all the chores. You may have heard the term, 'Women's work is never done'. Whoever said that must have been thinking of ranch women.

"In the summer the hay had to be cut and put in the barn for feed for the cows and horses during the winter months. Kay's Papa hired workers to help, but the family had to work, too. Mary, Kay's older sister, stayed on the hay wagon and rearranged the hay as it was tossed up from the field. She watched carefully, because sometimes a snake would be tossed in the wagon with the hay. Even Kay had a job. She led Dolly, the horse, as he pulled the cable which lifted the large hay loaded hay-fork into the barn.

"In the autumn the potatoes were dug up. It was exciting to pull up the plants from the soil and find beautiful large potatoes. It reminded her a bit of looking for Easter eggs, for you never knew what a plant would yield. Kay soon tired of digging potatoes and we would wander off to do more fun things.

"Having enough wood to last the winter was important. You needed wood to cook the food and heat the house. Trees were felled, and a water driven roundsaw cut the wood in desired lengths. Then the wood had to be chopped, the smaller pieces for the kitchen stove, and larger ones for the heating stove. It took a great deal of wood to supply the house, and the woodshed would be stacked to the ceiling.

" In the winter all of us cats spent most of our time in the barn under a blanket of hay.

"Winter was a time of contrasts. The barn and dairy had no heat. What a blessing it was to come into a warm kitchen after doing the early morning chores of feeding the animals and milking the cows.

"Kay loved to break off the long icicles which formed at the edge of the roof, and she would have a sword fight with her brother. She knew it was really cold when the milk in the glass bottles froze. The milk turned from a liquid into a solid which caused the cap from the bottle to pop off leaving a column of frozen milk that looked like a miniature popsicle.

"Winter was not a pleasant time at the ranch, because only the kitchen and dining room were heated. The bedrooms were like iceboxes. Since she was the smallest, Kay slept between her sisters, and with a warm body on each side of her, she did not feel the cold.

Grandma paused and drew a deep breath. She seemed to almost stop her story, but she continued. "One very cold, stormy February night Kay's dear Papa died of a heart attack. The snow was deep, and as you know, the ranch was four miles from town. Joe and his cousin, Chris, put Papa's body on the sled to be taken to town. Kay, with tears running down her face, put wool socks on her Papa's feet for she didn't want his feet to be cold.

"The boys took two teams of horses. One would go in the lead to clear the deep drifts of snow, and the team pulling the sled would follow. When one team became exhausted, Joe and Chris would unhitch them, and the horses would change places. It took many hours for the boys to arrive in town."

Grandma did not say another word, and the kittens crowded around her, trying to let her know how sorry they felt. It made them realize that life wasn't always fun, and there would be some sorrow in everyone's life.

GOURMET FOOD AT THE RANCH

Grandma Tabby welcomed the kittens with her usual warmth. How they loved her because she was fun and always kind. They thought surely she would run out of stories about Kay, but she started by saying, "Everyone at the ranch ate well.

"When Kay was a little girl she ate food that was considered gourmet. One reason was that her stepmother had been a cook at a fancy resort in Switzerland. Kay liked frog legs. I think what she really liked was catching the frogs in the irrigation ditch."

Calico interrupted, "I don't think frog legs sound like good food."

Grandma continued, "Kay said the legs tasted like tender chicken. Her brother, Joe, caught trout from the stream; if there were any fried trout left over they were marinated in wine vinegar and herbs. Kay liked that the best. But I liked my fish heads without vinegar.

"On Christmas Eve, Kay, with her sisters and brother, would be taken to town to attend the midnight church service. Kay told me that coming back to the ranch in the unheated milk truck was a very cold experience. Oh, during that time cars had no heaters either. But on arriving home they would find a pot of stewed tripe simmering on the stove. It was delicious. I was always given a taste. Kay said she has ordered tripe in restaurants, but it chewed like rubber and had no taste."

Grandma had a smile on her face as she told about Christmas. "On Christmas Day many wonderful smells would come from the kitchen. Kay spent a long time by the hot stove stirring risotto, for the meal would not be compete without this wonderful rice. It had to be cooked slowly with homemade chicken broth, a bit of white wine, and wild mushrooms which had been picked in the spring and dried.

"One strange custom was performed before the family sat down for their Christmas feast. Kay, at her stepmother's urging, had to take a large dish of this wonderful risotto to the chickens. It was to thank the chickens for all the eggs they had laid for the family. I would go to the chicken house with Kay and would hear her mutter, 'What a waste of good risotto.' But that was the custom in the small Italian village where her stepmother had grown up. Kay tells me that now in the city you can take cooking lessons which teach you how to make risotto."

Grandma wasn't finished yet. "At Easter there would be roasted kid which is a baby goat. Kay did not like to see it in the oven, because it reminded her of a naked baby. I tasted some and agreed with her that it was delicious. One of Kay's favorites was roasted pork ribs. The meat was crisp and tasty, and she always shared a rib with me.

"The cellar had shelves of several kinds of homemade cheese. The one that Kay could not stand was worm cheese. This was a type of cheese made without salt, and when it aged it developed worms. The only ones who ate it were the workmen. Kay would turn her head, so she wouldn't see them eat the wiggly worms.

"Kay told me that many years later she attended a Commonwealth Club meeting in San Francisco where her husband, Forest, was a member. The speaker was an author who spoke about his book which was titled, *Worms in my Father's Cheese*. After hearing him speak, Kay felt better knowing that others ate wormy cheese. I don't know why she didn't like it, because I tasted the worms, and they were delicious."

THE CHICKEN DISASTER

"One day, Kay's stepmother was going to town for the day. How happy Kay and her cousin Eda were for they would have a free day to themselves. But their faces fell when they were told they had to roast a chicken for the workmen's Sunday dinner. They did as she had instructed and put the chicken in the oven.

"They went outside to swing on the long cable swing that was tied to a large oak tree. Kay felt that if she pumped really hard, she could touch the sky. Sometimes she took me in her lap, and how I loved that!

"Suddenly Kay and Eda realized that they had been outside for some time, and the stove needed wood to keep the oven hot. As they neared the house, they smelled something awful. I had smelled the odor for some time. The girls said, *What can it be?* The smell in the kitchen was unbearable. A workman, who was close by, came when he heard their excited voices. He soon discovered the cause. The chicken had been plucked of its feathers, but the intestines had not been removed. The workmen took the smelly chicken and buried it in the field. Everyone had bread and cheese for Sunday dinner, but I wasn't happy because I loved the crisp skin of the baked chicken.

"That night the coyotes, who had a good sense of smell, came and dug up the chicken for a feast.

"When Kay's stepmother arrived back at the ranch, she wanted some of the leftover chicken. The workmen told her the girls had done such a wonderful job cooking it that every bit had been eaten. I don't think she believed them, but there was nothing she could do about it. Both Eda and Kay were grateful to the workmen, because they saved them from a scolding."

The kittens were hungry after hearing about the good food, but they were happy they hadn't been around to smell the chicken.

MILKING TIME AT THE RANCH

Today was going to be a special treat. Grandma had promised the kittens that she would tell them a story about their Uncle Whiskers. He was a wonderful uncle, and when he visited the kitten's mother, they heard all kinds of tales about his adventures. The kitten's mother wasn't always happy about that.

Grandma started her story: "On the ranch all of us cats lived in the barn, and it was our job to catch mice. There were lots of mice, because the grain for the chickens was stored in the barn, and you know how much mice love to eat grain. With the mice, and a saucer of fresh milk that Kay gave us each morning, we were very well-fed cats.

"Uncle Whiskers especially liked milking time. This happened very early in the morning and again in the afternoon. Uncle Whiskers had learned to position himself so that the milkers could squirt milk directly into his mouth. I have never seen any other cat who could do this. He especially liked it, because when the milk comes from the cow it is warm.

"Uncle Whiskers said it tasted very good, and he put on quite a show during milking time. Kay laughed wherever she saw him catch the milk in his mouth this way. After his show, he would leave the barn with his tail held high in the air.

"All this came to an end when milking machines replaced the hand milkers. No more milkers and no more show. Uncle Whiskers was depressed for some time, but soon his sunny nature came back, and we all loved being with him."

"That was a nice story, but it was too short," said Blackie.

Grandma continued, "I'll tell you about the time when we were all very frightened. It was in the middle of a bright sunny day. I was in the field hunting for mice, and all of a sudden it started to get dark. Soon it was dark as night, and I heard the rooster crow which never happens in the daytime. What was happening? I looked for Kay, and when I found her, she did not seem at all frightened. So I thought that whatever it is, it can't be too bad after all. I heard Kay say that what was happening was called a full eclipse of the sun. It lasted far longer than I liked, but little by little the sun did come back."

FAREWELL UNTIL NEXT SUMMER

"You know Grandma, when you started telling us the stories about the ranch, it sounded like a bit of heaven," said Calico, "but then when you think about it, we are all more comfortable now, especially in the winter. The modern appliances, such as the furnaces, the washers and the refrigerators are all taken for granted. People don't have to work as hard or as long at their housework. The ranch was a wonderful place, and I will never forget what I have learned about yours' and Kay's life, but I am happy that I am a modern cat."

Grandma smiled, "There are always two sides to every story. It was wonderful for Kay and me to wander unafraid over the countryside and to find a hill covered with Shasta lilies with their sweet smell permeating the entire area. Another thing I remember was that on a clear, dark night, I would look up at the unpolluted sky and see the Milky Way with its millions of stars in unbelievable brilliance."

The kittens nodded. They realized there was more to life than creature comforts."

Blackie, Calico, and Patches felt very fortunate to have a Grandma who knew so many interesting things and who could tell such fascinating stories. Not all kittens were as lucky as they were. Today was the kitten's last visit until next year. They were going home to the city with Claire and her family, but they knew they would be back next summer for more stories about Rainbow Ranch.